Brian Haggard

Embroidered Memories

375 Embroidery Designs • 2 Alphabets • 13 Basic Stitches
for Crazy Quilts, Clothing, Accessories...

C&T PUBLISHING

Text copyright © 2012 by Brian Haggard

Photography and Artwork copyright © 2012 by C&T Publishing, Inc.

Publisher: **Amy Marson**

Creative Director: **Gailen Runge**

Art Director: **Kristy Zacharias**

Editor: **Liz Aneloski**

Technical Editor: **Alison M. Schmidt**

Cover Designer: **April Mostek**

Book Designer: **Rose Sheifer**

Production Coordinator: **Zinnia Heinzmann**

Production Editor: **S. Michele Fry**

Illustrator: **Lon Eric Craven**

Photography by Christina Carty-Francis and Diane Pedersen of C&T Publishing, Inc., unless otherwise noted.

Published by C&T Publishing, Inc., P.O. Box 1456, Lafayette, CA 94549

Library of Congress Cataloging-in-Publication Data

Haggard, Brian.

Embroidered memories : 350 embroidery designs - 2 alphabets - 13 basic stitches - for crazy quilts, clothing, accessories... / Brian Haggard.

  pages cm

ISBN 978-1-60705-570-9 (soft cover)

1. Embroidery--Patterns. I. Title.

TT771.H15 2012

746.44--dc23

2012007866

Printed in China

10 9 8 7 6 5 4 3 2 1

Contents

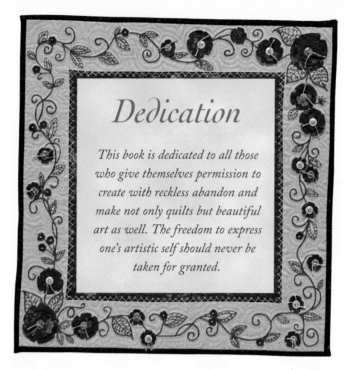

Dedication

This book is dedicated to all those who give themselves permission to create with reckless abandon and make not only quilts but beautiful art as well. The freedom to express one's artistic self should never be taken for granted.

Acknowledgments

I am thankful for the great success of my first book, *Crazy Quilted Memories*, and to all the many people who have asked me to make a pattern book. What you hold is a labor of love from my daydreaming.

First and foremost I want to thank my mother, Debbie, and my father, Rich, for their continued support and encouragement. I'm awed by my older brother, Shane, and his inspiring ongoing story of our family. Shane, you blow me away with your creative mind. My friend Janet Brandt is always a constant affirmation of what creativity is. She is truly an inspiration, and I thank her so much for all of her help in pushing me in the right direction. To my wonderful partner, Kevin Head, who always has that smile and a pat on the back to tell me that this is all worth it and to follow my dream—thank you, Kevin, for your undying support and for having my back in any situation. This year a person has entered my life, lent a hand, and given me so much inspiration—Judith Montano, I thank you from the bottom of my heart for all your mentoring and guidance. Your support will always mean the world to me. I must give a shout-out to a wonderful friend who has moved away but is by no means far from my heart—Melissa Taylor, not only do you and your quilting skills add to my work, but your wonderful support and friendship mean even more to me. This would not be a proper acknowledgment without recognizing the crazies from Arkansas—my friend, Sherry Ford; my best friend, Patricia Eaton; and let's not forget my very, very best friend, Jim Gatling (wink). You all have made my entrance into the quilting world a complete joy, and I thank you. I want to thank all of my stitching friends in my Wednesday stitch group for the laughs and support, especially the yo-yo queen, Sally Francis. If ever there is a group that keeps me grounded and motivated, it's all my good friends at The Back Door Quilts. Teri Dougherty, Linda Hale, and all the employees—two words: You rock! I can't say enough good things about the great people at C&T Publishing. I feel so fortunate to work with such a talented and thoughtful team. And the one person who has made this all a reality—Sandy Elliott, I thank you so much for all the hours of writing and editing and the use of such a brilliant mind. Your friendship is like nothing I've ever encountered. Thanks for all that is written on these pages; you have to know you make dreams happen. And last but certainly not least, my eternal gratitude goes to my grandmothers Juanita Lucille Carson Taylor and Opal Ester Richie Haggard and my great-grandmother Etta Mae Reid, who inspired me to create these great works. You will never be forgotten. Love to you all.

A Day in the Life of a Crazy-Quilt Artist

A story from the imagination of Shane Haggard for Brian Haggard

The early morning of fall combined with the warm ground of summer has swelled the air with fog. My editor just called to tell me that my first book, *Crazy Quilted Memories,* has gone international. Feeling a bit overwhelmed by the news, I have made my way to the grand porch with my coffee to take some time to reflect in the very spot where this journey started. Never in my wildest dreams did I think my book would be embraced by so many.

My great-great-grandmother would be so happy to learn that her legacy lives on. The months of digging for and restoring the items that once made her haberdashery so successful have been a labor of love, which is still a work in process. Using these finely worn and aged items to create projects has tethered our spirits for a lifetime. Over a year later I am still unearthing things from the attic tomb to share. I have been careful to explore closely every cobwebbed corner and dusty counter, as each holds a missing piece to the story of her life.

About six months into the sorting process I noticed a narrow beam of light stretching across the floor. It revealed a small space between two wooden slats on the wall. The dry wood had shrunk and uncovered a secret hiding place long forgotten. I gently pulled on the dried wood, and a small door swung open. Inside, a cavernous hideaway.

Covered in layers of time, a metal box in the middle of the room barely reflected the beam of the flashlight. The opening of the small forgotten room was just large enough to climb into. Inside, the walls were covered with pictures and

Photo by Kevin Head and Brian Haggard

French Mannequin

Inside was the most beautiful wooden French doll—
her hands and arms moved, so she could
be posed in various positions.

postcards from my grandmother's father during his travels. This was my grandmother's secret hideaway, where she must have dreamt of creating clothing and acted out her fantasies.

An Asian rug covered the cold, dusty floor. Small wooden hangers held antique clothes, obviously tailored by my grandmother for her dolls—each a miniature work of art, carefully crafted with love. Feeling a cord touching my head, I pulled gently. The room filled with light, and the dangling shade made of silk, now shredded by time, swung back and forth.

The metal box was much easier to see now, and my heart began to pound and my face flushed. It was heavy as I moved it closer to me, and I had to sit. What could be inside? Did I want to open it? Should I leave it as I found it? My curiosity, of course, won the battle. The lid creaked as I slowly opened the top. I got a sense of how my grandmother must have felt the first time she opened the box and saw what it revealed. Inside was the most beautiful wooden French doll—her hands and arms moved, so she could be posed in various positions. Her base flared to give her musty dress the illusion of fullness. I gently pulled her from the

box and blew several times to clean her face. Her paint had long been rubbed away from excessive love, but detailed carving in the wood revealed the delicate angelic face of the time. Her hand held the skeleton of a marionette in clothing identical to hers. It hung from the single thread that time had not claimed. Both dolls wore clothes of only the finest materials, embellished with lace and mother-of-pearl buttons. I carefully transported her to the dining room table to continue my exploration. She has since been moved from her time capsule and restored to her original beauty.

I share this story because it was and is my inspiration for this book. My grandmother lived in a time where functionality came first; style and fashion were secondary to all else. Items such as this doll were labors of love and a reminder to all to find their playful side. My grandmother would have wanted to see her items used to create functional pieces. Therefore, I have fashioned the items for this book to be functional, while maintaining a sense of the past and honoring my grandmother's findings. Remember to find the playfulness in all you do, and work it into the fibers and threads of your life.

Chapter 1

INTRODUCTION

Creativity is never born out of fear.

The need to design is what drives me. I love classic designs and patterns. With a nod to vintage style, I strive to make the new look old. Like a comfortable pair of shoes, it makes me happy. My desire in writing this book is to help release the inner artist inside everyone. When I teach, my students want me to draw on their quilts. But I want you to know, to believe, that you can create without copying. You can draw on your own quilts. Use the patterns in this book as a template to inspire you to create something uniquely your own.

The images in this book are here to inspire you— to start a creative flow in your mind. Don't allow them to stifle you by trying to follow them exactly. They are fluid. Release your imagination and let the images become what you want them to be.

Chapter 2

KEEPING THE HISTORY OF HAND EMBROIDERY ALIVE

Learning the history of hand embroidery is my new passion. Needle Fever has really gotten me. (Note: This is an epidemic.) History is a storytelling thing, and hand embroidery is part of that.

Since the fourteenth century, people have embroidered to acknowledge births, marriages, treasures, pets, and deaths. Elaborate handwork embellished the gowns of kings and queens. Stitchery was a pastime for women of wealth. The Victorian era saw a resurgence of hand embroidery. Luxurious fabrics such as silk and velvet were rare and highly sought-after commodities. Using hand embroidery was a resourceful way to make art pieces out of scraps of fine fabrics, perhaps left over from ball gowns. A woman might also use hand embroidery to make a personal gift for a dear friend or a betrothed, or gifts to celebrate holidays and weddings.

Excellent stitchery was a status symbol. If the lady of the house had fabulous needle skills and creativity, it was a distinguished feather in her cap.

Stitchery had a lot to do with teaching young girls to become adults. At ages six to eight, they began stitching on burlap sacks or linen towels to make samplers as learning tools to teach them many things, from the alphabet and numbers to Bible verses and lessons.

One of my favorite things is to use fragments of treasures in my quilting—in essence, adding history to my quilts.

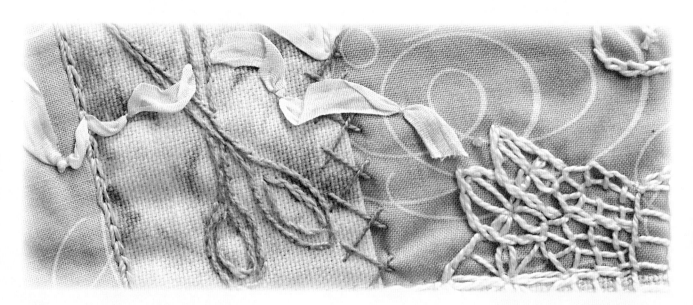

Chapter 3

BASIC STITCHES

All but one of these basic stitches can be created using assorted threads or ribbon (silk, cotton, or organza). I use #8 perle cotton for most of my embroidery. I love it because it rarely twists or tangles. If it does, I just hit it with a little bit of thread conditioner, such as Thread Heaven. However, the Japanese ribbon stitch can only be made with ribbon.

Instead of using a hoop to stabilize the quilt top I plan to embroider, I use Shape-Flex (a woven fusible material available from C&T Publishing and most fabric shops). I prepare my quilt top by turning it facedown to start. I cut strips of Shape-Flex that are about an inch wider than the finished width of the sashing strips and adhere them with an iron onto the back of the quilt, covering the sashing and overlapping the crazy-pieced areas on either side of the seam.

If you worry about the edges of pieced seams opening up, you can do one of two things—serge around the edges or use a zigzag stitch with a ¼″ seam allowance to temporarily bind it all together.

Try different sizes and types of needles to see what you like best. I mainly use sharps (which are also called embroidery needles) with a large eye. For heavy fabrics such as upholstery and home décor fabrics, I use calico braiding needles, which have a sharp, triangular shaft to more easily pierce the material. For ribbon embroidery, use a large-eyed needle; just make an angled cut at the beginning of the piece of ribbon, and it will slide right through the eye.

Soft Knot

A soft knot on the back of the work will stay close to the fabric, will not misshape the project, and will not leave running threads on the back. If you're mixing threads, they can catch on the back and create a mess. When designs get complex, you don't want to sew through all those running threads.

1. Come up at A (on the back side of the project) and wrap the thread over the top of the needle to create a loop.

2. Pull the needle and thread in one direction and the loop in the other direction to create a Y.

3. Place your finger in the middle of the Y and pull the thread through until it finishes in a knot under your nail.

4. Trim the thread about ¼″ from the knot.

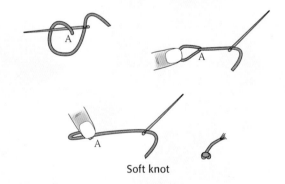

Soft knot

French Knot

Uses of the French knot are endless. What a versatile stitch! It's great for creating flower centers, clusters of grapes, texture to fill an area around flowers, baby's breath from a featherstitch, and so much more. You will want to add this stitch to your repertoire.

1. Come up at A and wrap the thread twice around the needle.

2. While tilting the needle one way and holding the thread the other way, go down at B (as close to A as possible) and keep the thread close to the fabric.

3. Hold the knot in place while pulling the needle through the fabric.

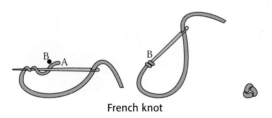

French knot

Chain Stitch

You can make this stitch in any direction—up or down, left or right. You can also shape it to fit a curved line.

1. Come up at A and go down at B (close to A). Make a loop and hold the loop in place with your thumb. Come up at C inside the loop. Always keep the loop to the forward point of the needle so you can direct the loop along the line you want to travel.

2. Pull the needle taut, but not so tight that you lose the nice soft loop. Create the same stitch again, but this time do it inside the loop to continue the chain.

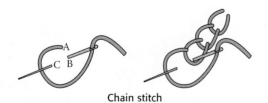

Chain stitch

Lazy Daisy

I love to use lazy daisy flowers with button embellishments and French knots in the center.

1. Come up at A and go down at B (close to A). Make a loop and hold the loop in place with your thumb. Come up at C. (However large you want the daisy petal to be is how far you want to travel, usually ⅛″–¼″.)

2. Pull and leave a nice loopy, billowed arch to create a petal.

3. Go straight down on the other side of the loop at D, creating a small stitch to tack the loop in place. You've now made your first daisy petal. Go back to the center to create more of these in concentric shapes and make as many petals as you want.

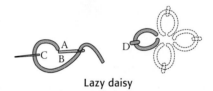

Lazy daisy

Brian's Y Stitch, aka Fly Stitch

Seldom will you use this stitch by itself, but in combination it's a great tool to tie many stitches together.

1. Come up at A, go down at B, and come up at C.

2. Cross under the first stitch and go down at D, creating a Y.

The modified Y stitch, or star stitch, is the same as the Y stitch but with a short stem to create the star effect.

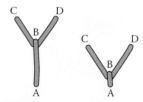

Y stitch and modified Y stitch

Brian's Asterisk

Use this stitch to incorporate background texture and patterns or to make flowers. It's very simple, yet very effective.

1. Make 2 straight stitches across each other to create a cross.

2. Add 2 straight stitches to make an X across the cross, creating the asterisk.

3. Bring the needle up in the center of the asterisk and take a tack stitch across all 4 threads.

Brian's asterisk

Buttonhole Stitch

The buttonhole stitch is one of the most versatile stitches you will learn. By varying the size and direction, you can create many things from this one marvelous stitch. I use it to appliqué for a primitive look, to outline, or to add ornamental stitching to seams. Stitch at an angle to create a fern effect.

1. Come up at A and travel over and down at B. Hold the thread between A and B loosely, and come up at C.

2. Repeat, pulling each stitch evenly taut. Keep the stitches even and in a straight line.

Buttonhole stitch

Stem and Outline Stitches

Use these stitches to write or to make intricate lines.

1. Come up at A, take a small stitch, and go down at B; then come up at C, about halfway back to A.

2. Travel half a stitch, go down at D, and come up at E (right next to B). Continue, keeping the thread on the bottom and the needle on top to make an even stem. Always make sure the thread is on the same side of the needle as you travel. If the thread is kept above or *over* the needle (remember the "o"), you are making an outline stitch. If the thread is kept below the needle (as drawn), it is a stem stitch. The end result looks the same.

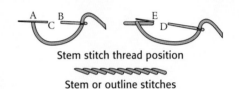

Stem stitch thread position

Stem or outline stitches

Cretan Stitch

This even stitch creates a nice balance down a center seam.

1. Imagine 3 vertical lines. (If this is a new stitch for you, go ahead and draw 3 vertical lines on your fabric with a removable marking tool, such as a chalk pencil or a FriXion pen, page 17.) Come up at A. Make a stitch from B to C, with the thread under the needle and without stitching all the way to the centerline.

2. Pull the thread through. Make the next stitch the same as in Step 1, but go down at D and come up at E (from left to right).

3. Repeat Steps 1 and 2, alternating from side to side.

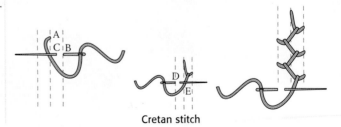

Cretan stitch

Featherstitch

This is one of my favorite stitches to use in crazy quilts. It helps create the Old World style. It's also versatile. But be aware—it's a directional stitch! The line does not have to be straight. You also could follow a seam, which is where this stitch is most prominently used in quilts. Following a seam-line helps keep the stitches straight and consistent.

1. Come up at A, go down at B, and come up at C.

2. Alternate the stitches back and forth on each side of an imaginary line.

Featherstitch

The double featherstitch is created the same as the featherstitch; you just do 2 stitches before alternating on either side of the imaginary line.

To form a triple featherstitch, guess what? Just do 3 stitches before alternating on either side of the imaginary line!

Chevron Stitch

This unique stitch can be combined with other stitches to create many looks.

1. Come up at A, go down at B, and come up at C, in the middle between A and B.

2. Travel downward across the seam, go down at D, come up at E, and go down at F.

3. Come back up at G and travel up to H. You've now created the first chevron. Start over at the next position A to create the next chevron.

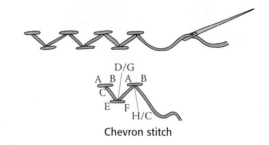

Chevron stitch

Tip

If you have a hard time seeing where the stitches should be, draw sets of three dots as a guide on your fabric.

Chevron stitch variations with French knots, straight stitches, and lazy daisies

Herringbone Stitch

The herringbone stitch is a very Old World stitch. You will find it on very early quilts. It creates a crosshatch style of overlapping X's. This is an excellent stitch to use for seams, but it also can be used to create many other motifs.

1. Come up at A, go down at B (crossing the seam), come up at C, cross over the thread between A and B (which creates the X), and go down at D. You have now created the first stitch.

2. Come up at the next position A; repeat all the steps through D, alternating from side to side across the seam. Each time you repeat this sequence, you will have another herringbone stitch for the seam.

The most important thing to remember as you make this stitch is the evenness on each side of the seam. If you are like me, you will tend to get more relaxed as you stitch, and the stitches will stretch out.

Japanese Ribbon Stitch

When making the Japanese ribbon stitch, you will want to use *only* silk ribbon specifically designed for embroidery. If you are new to silk ribbon embroidery, I have some quick tips to get you started:

Unwind about 20″ of ribbon and cut it on the diagonal. Thread this cut end through a large-eyed needle. Using the same end, pierce the ribbon about ¼″ from the end with the tip of the needle. Pull the needle one way and the ribbon the other. Pull the ¼″ tail over the eye of the needle. You have now "locked on."

By doing this you are creating a single ribbon to pull through the fabric so you do not wear out the ribbon by doubling it over.

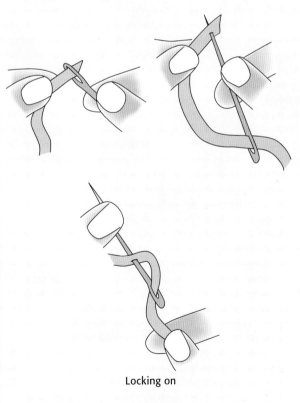

Locking on

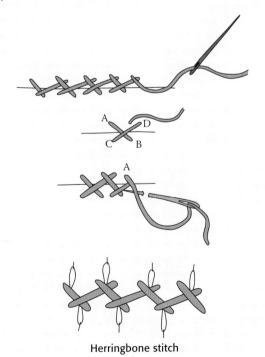

Herringbone stitch

Next, create a circle by positioning the tip of the needle as if it were kissing the other end of the ribbon.

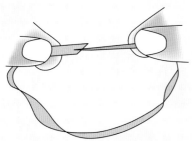

"Kissing" with the needle and the ribbon

Make 3 small stitches through the ribbon with the tip of the needle. Holding the tip of the needle, pull the gathered ribbon past the eye of the needle, pulling to the end of the ribbon. You have now created a soft knot and can start stitching. **WARNING**: You will now be addicted to silk ribbon embroidery.

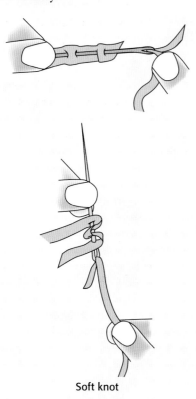

Soft knot

1. Come up at A. With your thumb, place the silk ribbon parallel to where you want the foliage or petal to go.

2. Pierce the ribbon with your needle at B and pull gently to the back until the ribbon turns in gracefully on itself, making the first Japanese ribbon stitch.

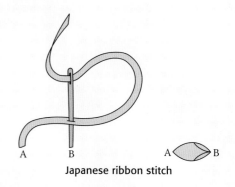

Japanese ribbon stitch

Use multiple Japanese ribbon stitches to create foliage and flowers, as shown. This is a useful stitch!

Japanese ribbon stitch variations

Chapter 4

Drawing Elements:

EVOLUTION OF A DESIGN

For me, the evolution of a design really starts with an oddly shaped area that needs to be filled or an area in a quilt that runs across seamlines. So, as in all things that I do, there are no hard-and-fast rules. Generally, I like to start with the largest object in the design, for example, a circle or a button, and let everything else satellite out from that object. Whether I follow a vertical line or a horizontal line or create a starburst effect around the object doesn't matter. I can create a flower bouquet or any other design element that is cohesive and has eye appeal.

I like to hand draw designs and let them evolve. I might start with some circles clustered together in a triangle, and then add some leaves and curlicues. This is a great way to fill an odd space and make the design look like it's meant to be there.

A floral motif or a grouping on a quilt needs to have an element that will fill the space available. I like to start in the center and work out. Sometimes I freehand it and create with the needle as I go. Other times, I draw only small lines to get me started. Most of the elements in this book are meant for you to use as a framework, not for you to create the exact same thing. For example, if you use one of the circle designs, you can make that circle in many different ways. You may even wish to scan and scale it or any of the images up or down on your computer. Look at the projects in the gallery for inspiration.

I may use silk flowers, buttons, bows, ribbon, silk ribbon, embroidery floss, or any crazy combination of these and other things I find. I certainly don't limit myself to one or two items. I use it all! See how I used an actual miniature glove (below)? It makes a great companion for a flower. Now the glove looks like it's holding something.

Miniature glove and antique bird toy from *Tattered Fragments of Friends* (page 63)

I also like to use found objects—things that are lying around. One of the things I get the most questions about is a small barbell with bells on the ends of it that was given to me by a friend. We didn't know what it was and were delighted when we discovered it is an antique toy for a bird to peck and play with. I wrapped ribbon around it and sewed it on *Tattered Fragments of Friends* (page 15) to create a cute little charm.

I used a lot of hands in my projects for this book. Some of them are holding items; I like that look. It's my variation on the traditional heart-in-hand design, a kind of Old World brought to the New.

The evolution of a design should start with a small, simple motif and grow to where you want it. Allow it to happen. Don't look at my designs just as they are. Use them as tools to create with by adding embellishments, making them bigger or smaller,

or taking things away you don't want and adding things you do. My designs are only guidelines—a place from which to launch the artist in you. I find it humorous when my students say, "I don't like the scroll going in that direction." I tell them time and again, "It's your quilt. Work with it. Make it your own. That's why they call it 'crazy.' There are no rules here. Remember, this is me we're talking about."

This is about having fun, being playful, and creating with what you have. Showing you how to create my exact quilt is not the purpose of this book. You won't have all the elements I have; I wouldn't have all the elements you have. It's about found objects and you enjoying them. One of my favorite places to dig for things to inspire me is Grandma's button tin. Not only will I find buttons in there, but sometimes I'll find many other useful

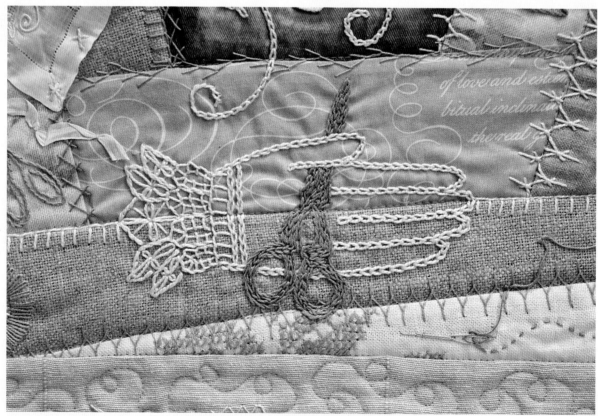

Chain-stitched scissors from *Florence's Haberdashery* (page 64)

things that are quite fun to use, such as snaps, bone trim from undergarments, skeleton keys, and so on. I found a pair of scissors and traced around them on *Florence's Haberdashery* (page 16). I chainstitched the tracing, and now it looks like a pair of scissors is on the quilt. I loved using this idea to cross the seamlines and create something lying on the quilt that doesn't have to be in the small framework within the seams.

This book will be a great success to me if you enjoy the process of making the project and love the outcome when it's finished. That's all I ask. Create with what you have. Whether you choose for the work to be as involved as mine or not as involved as mine, it's up to you as the artist. (For Pete's sake! This is not rocket science!)

I have many friends who are amazing stitchers and have unique styles. One is Judith Montano, the "Queen of Embroidery." I love her beautifully detailed embellishments and use of color. But I can't be Judith. I have to be me. Allie Aller is another friend who is a totally different type of crazy quilter, and yet I love her style, too. I can admire these women and their art. I can use and create from their art, but I can't be who they are nor can I do what they do. I must find and follow my own muse, and I want you to do the same.

The evolution of a design should be dictated by your creativity and not by the quilt piece itself. Be open to everything around you. You may find lace trims, buttons, or other elements that send you in a direction you never anticipated. That's okay. There are so many things to do, or change, or use in a new way. It makes each day different, and you won't get bored. If you look at it this way and go out into the world knowing that anything can be put on a quilt, you will have a totally new, open feeling

I must find and follow my own muse, and I want you to do the same.

about where your quilts will go next. I think the hunt and the chase for those items that are going to make your quilt special are part of what makes this whole experience worthwhile.

I used to use graphite pencils to draw on my projects, but once I drew on the fabric, it was pretty much permanent, whether I liked it or not. Then I discovered the FriXion pen by Pilot. It's one of my new favorite things! It's an erasable ballpoint pen that is just the bomb! When you hang out with people at quilt shops, you learn the craziest things. I was at my favorite quilt shop, Back Door Quilts, and they told me about this new ballpoint pen that you could use to write and draw on a quilt and then "erase" it with heat. I'm absolutely thrilled with this product! If you make a mistake, it's not a big deal. You just heat set it with an iron and it goes away. (I say "heat set" here and in my classes, even though I really mean "heat erase." You get the idea.) You can change the design and never see the old one, so you're never stuck. You can even use it to draw guidelines for precise stitching of the cretan or chevron stitches (not that I do). It's fabulous! I'm going to be the next Oprah! I've got my own favorite-things list!

Note

Be very careful when you go to erase FriXion pen ink with your iron. Don't touch any of the little pieces of the drawing or writing that you want to keep. I've learned this from sad experience, having had some great motifs eaten up by the heat of the iron. You might have luck getting your image back by freezing the fabric. You also could try using an appliqué iron to erase anything you don't like—the smaller head makes it easier to get in tight spots.

If you want to have family members sign their names, add their dates of birth, or draw something on your project, just hand them the FriXion pen and let them do it. After you have embroidered over it, you have essentially preserved their handwriting. It's a wonderful way to get that archival feel.

You can find FriXion pens at your local quilt shop or office supply store. There are no instructions on the package for use on fabric; you just start writing or drawing. The pens come in blue, red, black, and other assorted colors. Surprisingly, the pink shows up well on darker fabrics!

Note

Don't use FriXion pens on legal documents because you may be writing your name with something that doesn't last. It says right on the package that these pens are not recommended for legal signatures.

The only downside I've heard about the FriXion pen is that if it gets too cold, the ink could reappear after it's been erased. But you can easily put an iron to it and make it disappear again. Although this hasn't happened to me, it did give me an idea. Wouldn't it be cute to write a message on a project you're giving to a loved one and then heat the message to make it disappear? You could include a note telling the person to put it in the freezer so that he or she can find a secret message from you. I'm toying with that idea.

Chapter 5

HOW TO TRANSFER THE DESIGNS

As you talk with different stitch groups, quilters, and crafters, you find out about different ways of doing the same thing. Transferring designs is a perfect example. Some people like to trace a design on tissue paper, place it on top of the fabric, and then stitch through it. Others trace the image directly onto their fabric.

My favorite way to transfer embroidery designs to a project for stitching is to use Wash-Away Stitch Stabilizer (C&T Publishing). Wash-Away Stitch Stabilizer is a paper specifically made for transferring designs from a computer to fabric. It's easy to use and fast. Photocopy, or scan and print, the design you want onto a sheet of Wash-Away Stitch Stabilizer. Trim close to the design. Then position the design where you want it on your project. You can easily stitch through the Wash-Away Stitch Stabilizer. When you've finished your stitching, simply wet the stabilizer, and it dissolves.

One of the things I love about using Wash-Away Stitch Stabilizer is that you can peel it off and reposition the designs if you don't like where they are. You need to be somewhat decisive, though. You can't peel it off over and over again or it won't stick very well for you to stitch through. Remember, it's only a quilt. Work with it. Make it happen.

1. Pick an image from the book you want to use.

2. Photocopy or scan the image (enlarge, reduce, or alter as you wish).

3. Print a test on a piece of computer paper.

4. Put an 8½″ × 11″ sheet of Wash-Away Stitch Stabilizer into the printer.

5. Print.

6. Cut close to the image. (Be sure to leave the backing paper on until you're ready to position the image on your project.)

7. Audition all the pieces you plan to use to ensure that you're happy with the placement of the designs.

8. Carefully peel off the backing paper.

9. Place the stabilizer with the design on the project where you want it. You can reposition it a time or two.

10. Stitch through the Wash-Away Stitch Stabilizer and the project.

 *Note*

Make sure you do a test print on the Wash-Away Stitch Stabilizer to ensure that your printer's black ink will not bleed onto your quilt when you wet the Wash-Away Stitch Stabilizer to dissolve it. If it does, use light-colored ink. I like sepia brown because it matches the fabrics I use. Choose a pale color and make sure it will not bleed onto your fabric. Soft gray or soft brown inks work well for white fabrics. Change the ink color by using the color palette in your photo-editing software. I use Picasa. It's a free Google download I use to do my photo editing.

Set forth and conquer the fear of your inner artist with needle in hand, an open heart, and a creative mind! Grab your needles, line up your threads, gather your vintage finds, and just start designing!

Chapter 6

EMBROIDERY DESIGNS

FLORAL *Banners and heart*

Floral banners

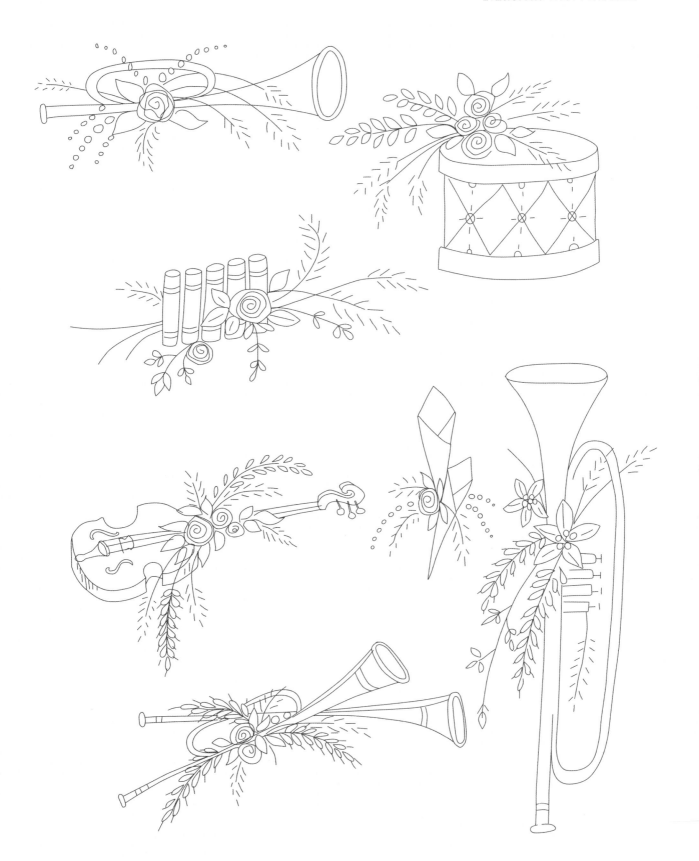

Luck be with you

CLASSIC *Cookie-cutter creation*

Classic circles

Berry bonanza

MULTI MOTIFS

Elongated designs

Classical Shelly

Sushi's appearance (cat)

GALLERY

Letters of Remembrance

The border on *Letters of Remembrance* is the main color that's carried throughout the whole piece. The floral motif on the border is hand drawn and decorated with buttons given to me by a dear friend in the form of napkin rings. I took them apart and used the buttons throughout the quilt. All the motifs reflect items used to sit down and write a letter—a pair of glasses at your desk, a clock to tell the time, an ink blotter, quill pens, and ink well.

A Visit to St. Mary's

This crazy quilt is about hand-dyed fabrics, laces, and trims used in different ways. I used die-cut flowers to create the large motif on the right side. I made small patchwork squares in each corner—all different, to make it more interesting. This project was used for a retreat I did with some students at Saint Mary-of-the-Woods College in Indiana. I must say they did me proud.

Vintage Garden

This crazy quilt is stitched with unique flora and fauna designs. The basket serves as a center motif, and the bird carrying a banner makes an unexpected and fun place to stitch a date. The border was worked by hand after being pieced. I used buttons for accents throughout.

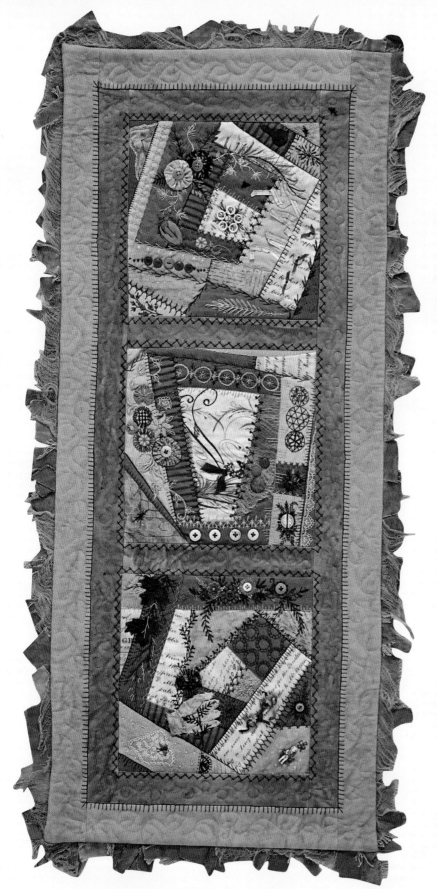

This is a three-block crazy quilt with tattered edges. Each block contains unique elements.

The top block has flowers made from fabric yo-yos. The lower yo-yo is pulled from its original shape to make a cute little bloom. Notice the flowers in the center. These are made from bone pieces taken from vintage ladies' lingerie. I put them together to look like the center of a flower. See the small paper fragments that are sandwiched in the seam? It's a new thing I'm trying. I love the phrase "Live with passion!" In the corner is a wonderful little key given to me by my dear friend Sally. (Sally also makes yo-yos for me.) A little bee is caught in the cobweb in the upper right of the block, and if you look closely, you can see that one has escaped!

The middle block has a swan motif. I added a yo-yo and various laces to make the floral motif on the left side. There are vegetable ivory buttons for trim. I stitched some unique repetitive patterns. Sometimes I do that to make a nice flow while not overpowering the piece by having too many motifs close together.

The third block has a wonderful little garden glove stitched to it. I embroidered a single-stem flower on top to make it look like it's held in the glove. To the right of the glove is the little barbell bird toy (page 15). At the top of this block is a favorite motif of mine made with French knots, lazy daisies, and Japanese ribbon stitches. The way it's put together makes it unique, even ethereal, to me. The leaves are die cut from fabric with two pieces sandwiched together and then appliquéd. The little German doll in the lower right corner is called a Frozen Charlotte.

Tattered Fragments of Friends

Florence's Haberdashery

The beautiful lady in this picture is Florence Kelly, who came to me through a student, Kathleen Hash. I was so fond of the picture that I asked Kathleen if I could use it. That is how I found out that Florence, Kathleeen's grandmother, born in 1884, was an avid embroiderer, a seamstress, and a haberdasher. She said her grandmother would have been honored to be in this book. I thank Kathleen for sharing her family story. A lovely lady's hankie caresses Florence from the left edge of the photograph. You'll find all kinds of sewing implements embroidered throughout the piece. There's a beautiful gloved hand holding a pair of scissors, embroidered spools of thread, thimbles, a dressmaker's form, pairs of scissors, buttons, safety pins—things you'd find in a haberdashery. That's the story of my instant ancestor, Florence, because I've adopted her into my family.

Detail of *Florence's Haberdashery*

Detail of *Florence's Haberdashery*

Ava's Gift from Grandma

Yes, I can work with color! Colleen Bone was a dear friend I'd known for many years. The night before she passed, she asked me to come to her home and sit by her bedside. She asked me if I would please make this small crazy quilt for Ava Shepard, her granddaughter. The pictures in the quilt are of Ava; her mother, Heather Shepard; and Colleen. There's a small outline of Ava's hand, and in the center of the hand is a little heart with Ava's signature at age four. This quilt is a gift to Ava from her grandma. Colleen always liked a good joke, and she got me again. She told me she had all the fabrics for the quilt, and she had picked neutrals for me. When I got the bag of fabrics, it was filled with all these brilliant colors! I added the brown to tone it down. Everything else was in the bag. It was a personal joke between the two of us. I can imagine her still chuckling. I miss you, Colleen.

Fifteenth-Century Farthingale Bag, front

Fifteenth-Century Farthingale Bag, back

The lovely regal lady holding the back of a chair has been turned into a lady holding vines and floral pieces. A beautiful hat with an embroidered feather has been added to her head. Each piece was embroidered, and then the pieces were made into this lovely bag with a pocket where you can place your hand in the front. It holds your sewing implements and is meant to hang off your belt. The lady of the house would have worn this and carried all of her more important things with her, so they wouldn't be left lying around the house for servants to take. I love the collection of little pearl buttons that my dear friend Carol Bradley from my button group gave me. It was wonderful to have all these textures and likenesses together for this piece—very charming. Small silk pieces were tied at the bottom and knotted on with embroidery floss to make a wonderful fringe on the bottom of this bag.

Crazy Clutch, **front**

The Crazy Clutch was made out of a basic handle I found at a craft store. I chipped and distressed the paint to make it look old. I saw all these scraps lying on my bench and was inspired to put them together, which turned out to be quite fun. The small floral motif pieces spring from and circle center flowers. I also used linear-design flowers, such as the hollyhock. On the back is a medallion made from a piece of eyelet lace I cut out and stitched through. It adds a charming bit of detail. The bow has been pressed down and tackstitched to the clutch, carrying through the whole look of pearls, lace, and trims, appliquéd with many other things using perle cotton.

Crazy Clutch, **back**

Linen jacket, front

Detail of linen jacket

This is a Liz Claiborne jacket reclaimed from a consignment store. I replaced the plain pocket flaps with crazy-quilt pocket flaps. Then, I embellished the collar with eyelet pieces, which I attached with embroidery. Big time-saver! I've been told this is cheating. I don't think so. I call it working smart versus working hard. I cut out the lace appliqués on the pockets and dyed them to create this old and weathered look. The strap across the back has a tape measure, flower motifs, and premade lace pieces that were dyed. The infant picture of my dear grandmother Juanita Taylor is in the center. The close-up of the cuff demonstrates how adding laces, buttons, and trims together with perle cotton creates an overall cohesive, even ethereal, look from disparate things.

Detail of linen jacket, front

Detail of linen jacket, back

Grandma Opal's Tote

This is a small tote bag featuring a picture of my paternal grandma, Opal Haggard. She's holding a small pair of stork scissors. The group of antique caramel buttons on the top right helps build small motifs to create a new image, with overlays of lace, using a sandwiching effect. A 10˝ lined block is stitched to the front of the tote, creating a pocket. This is a quick, easy way to make a neat gift that is meaningful.

Quilter's Chatelaine

Detail of *Quilter's Chatelaine*

This is my alternative to wearing a tie at quilt shows, which I'm against. If I'm going to wear something around my neck, I want it to be useful. The chatelaine has pockets for scissors and a pen. There are two pockets on the back for business cards. One is for my business cards to give to others. The other is for business cards I've received. I used a little bit of everything in this. You'll find an old tape measure, embroidery, appliqué, an antique doily, a thread winder, buttons—lots of unique things.

Chair—A Token of My Affection

Detail of *Chair—A Token of My Affection*

This chair is in my design room. I covered it in linen and used it as a backdrop for the photographs of my three grandmothers. In the center is my grandmother Juanita Taylor. On the right is my great-grandmother Etta Mae Reid. On the left is my grandmother Opal Haggard. These are the three grandmothers I grew up with, and I always knew they had my back—they still do, in their new life on the other side. Their names and dates are embroidered on the back of the chair, along with photographs of memorabilia and items that all have sentimental value to me because they belonged to my grandmothers. It's something I get to live with and cherish every day. It's a living, working piece of art. But don't sit on it, please!

Detail of *Chair—A Token of My Affection*

French Mannequin

Photos by Kevin Head and Brian Haggard

decided to leave the wig off my form to give her quirkiness. Not a simple mannequin, she's a cage doll. A cage doll was used in French life to show dresses in miniature so a lady could decide whether she would like to have one in her own size. My grandmother Opal Haggard's high school diploma is on the mannequin's hip.

Detail of *French Mannequin*, back

Detail of marionette

The dress form is made of a wire sculpture from a French farthingale. I found out that the farthingale originated in Spain and migrated toward France. Marie Antoinette would have worn a farthingale, and this is made in that likeness. The gauze on the dress is dyed with Brian's Aging Mist. The rest of the dress is made of remnants of all kinds of wonderful things. You'll see all sorts of fun sewing implements on the doll. She's fun and fanciful. And she has a cute miniature marionette in her own likeness hanging in front of her.

The mannequin is done in French-court lifestyle. The women of the court would have shaved their heads and worn wigs. I

Millefleur Table Runner

This table runner was created using many of the motifs from the floral designs (pages 20–33). I started with a conical shape and began filling it in with circles to create a point. I then used leaves to fill in between and added a small fern blade where it was needed to create this delicate shape. The options are endless. Think of using this deisgn on the back of a blouse or on the lapel of a jacket to create a bouquet of flowers. Enjoy your creations!

Detail of *Millefleur Table Runner*

Briarpatch Floral Needle Case

Inside of *Briarpatch Floral Needle Case*

Briarpatch Floral Glasses Case

Briarpatch Floral Scissors Sheath

This is one of the many designs that you can create from the pages of individual floral motifs (pages 20–33), which include many types of leaves, foliage, and flowers. The only limit is your imagination. The small tongue made of two pieces of linen with fusible between them allows for easy storage of threads and needles.

Sometimes a motif does not have to be too involved. As shown here, a single flower and a few leaves placed appropriately can be very effective.

I like to create small pockets to hold my scissors and eyeglasses. It's a great way to transport them in a safe, easy manner. I chose to leave all the pocket edges raw to create a timeworn feel, even though it's a new piece.

Briarpatch Floral Sewing Sachet

This small purselike pouch can be used for any purpose you want. I created it featuring sewing notions to show how you can travel to your next sewing adventure in style. This is a great one-night project to give to a friend for a special occasion. Create your own floral motif with all the elements you have been given. Good luck!

Ms. Johneva Campbell's Inspiration

My dear friend Johneva Campbell loaned me this beautiful sewing bird for my last book. I loved the pictures of it so much that I created a small block with it as the centerpiece. The day Johneva brought me the sewing bird she also wowed me with an 1860s crazy quilt to use for ideas. And, boy, did I! This color palette is derived from her quilt. I cut the circle motifs from a penny-rug fabric. Look closely and you'll see that no two are alike. What a nice diversion from my usual color palette.

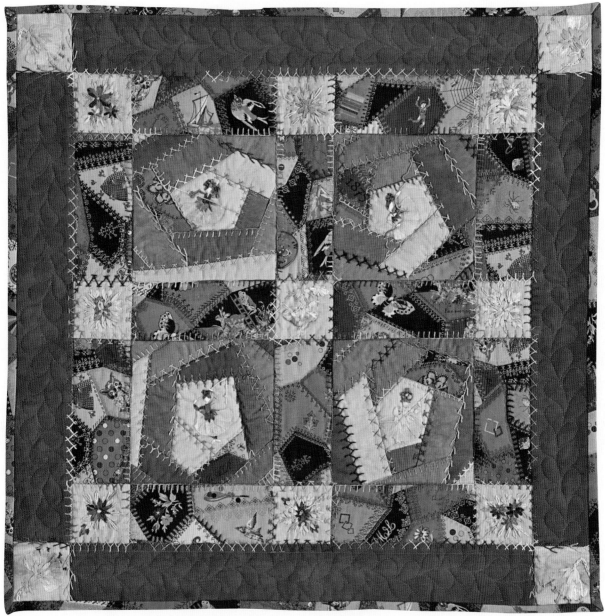

Playful Pixies

This quilt was inspired by some wonderful packets of hand-dyed fabrics from Cherrywood Fabrics, one of my favorite fabric makers. Then, I found the playful print. I thought how fun it would be to have these playful pixies in the center of each crazy-quilt block, pulling on the thread as if they were quilting fairies. The fairies materialized from the organza silk ribbon I hand dyed, making the floral blooms into the fairies' dresses. You'll notice that there's been a little detour off the path from my normal style and palette.

Little Lord Gatling

Be inspired to work smart instead of hard. The center of this quilt was pieced with many different colors of linen. While shopping with a client, I found this striped fabric by an absolute fluke, in the home dec department. It has every color of the linens I was using. I made the borders with the striped fabric and then embroidered over the seams to make it look pieced. Always remember to shop all the departments in your fabric store. I often find the most playful fabrics outside the quilting area.

Photo by Kevin Head and Brian Haggard

About the Author

Brian Haggard has never been one to be held to other people's ideas. His creative nature inspires people to try new things with found objects and to always look at them in new ways. He uses this gift in his interior design business, as he creates homes out of houses. Now, he has brought his unique perspective to the artistry of quilting.

At a young age, Brian was given a sewing machine by his parents, from which many projects were born. His pastime was making handcrafted items, with inspiration coming from just about anything in the universe. It has been a natural progression for him to create the textile works in this book.

His one wish, if you learn anything from the books that he writes, is that you be inspired to find your own creative genius and never forget to enjoy the process.

Brian is the current president of the Indianapolis Button Club. In addition to his love of buttons, he is always open to new ideas and new concepts and has been inspired to build many diverse collections—parts of which end up in his textile art and quilts. His greatest joy comes from the students he teaches and the smiles that cross their faces when they've freed their inner artist. Brian lives and works in Indianapolis in a newly designed loft-style studio.

Check out Brian's website, www.brianhaggard.com, for classes and retreats at The Haberdashery Studio & Retreat Center, and Brian's Aging Mist. See www.windhamfabrics.com for information about his fabric lines with Windham Fabrics.

Brian's Favorites

For the best fabrics and first-class service visit my friends at
The Back Door
2503 Fairview Place, Suite W
Greenwood, IN 46142
317-882-2120
www.backdoorquilts.com

My own fabric lines are produced and distributed by Windham Fabrics
(866) 842-7631
www.windhamfabrics.com

If you want the very best hand-dyed solids, I recommend Cherrywood Fabrics
888-298-0967
www.cherrywoodfabrics.com

Transform your fabric from pristine to timeworn with Brian's Aging Mist
www.brianhaggard.com

Keep an eye on Brian's website for the current classes and retreats at
The Haberdashery Studio & Retreat Center
2028 E. Southport Road
Indianapolis, IN 46227
www.brianhaggard.com

Also by author

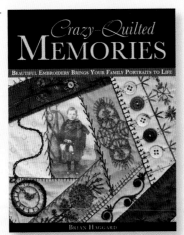

Great Titles *from* C&T PUBLISHING

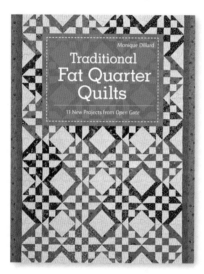

Available at your local retailer or **www.ctpub.com** *or* **800-284-1114**

For a list of other fine books from C&T Publishing, visit our website
to view our catalog online.

C&T PUBLISHING, INC.
P.O. Box 1456
Lafayette, CA 94549 | Email: ctinfo@ctpub.com
800-284-1114 | Website: www.ctpub.com

C&T Publishing's professional photography services are now available to
the public. Visit us at www.ctmediaservices.com.

Tips and Techniques can be found at www.ctpub.com > Consumer
Resources > Quiltmaking Basics: Tips & Techniques for Quiltmaking & More

For quilting supplies:

COTTON PATCH
1025 Brown Ave.
Lafayette, CA 94549
Store: 925-284-1177
Mail order: 925-283-7883 | Email: CottonPa@aol.com
| Website: www.quiltusa.com

Note: Fabrics shown may not be currently available, as fabric
manufacturers keep most fabrics in print for only a short time.